THE WAY LIFE WAS

A Chanticleer Press Edition

Compiled and written by
Jeffrey Simpson
Design and Coordination:
Massimo Vignelli and
Gudrun Buettner

First Edition 1974

Library of Congress Cataloging in Publication Data
Simpson, Jeffrey, comp.
The way life was.

1. United States—Civilization—1865–1918—
Pictorial works.   I. Title.
E169.1.S5883   917.3′03′80222   73–22526
ISBN 0–275–51670–9

Printed and bound by Amilcare Pizzi, S.p.A., Milan,
Italy

Prepared and produced by Chanticleer Press, Inc.
Staff for this book:
Publisher: Paul Steiner
Editor in Chief: Milton Rugoff
Managing Editor: Gudrun Buettner
Associate Editor: Susan Weiley
Production: Emma Staffelbach, Roberta Savage

Design: Massimo Vignelli

THE WAY LIFE WAS

**A Photographic Treasury from
the American Past**
by Chansonetta Emmons,
Frances Benjamin Johnston,
Alice Austen, Jacob Riis, The Byrons,
Lewis Hine, Henry Hamilton Bennett,
Solomon Butcher, L. W. Halbe,
Joseph Pennell, E. J. Bellocq,
Erwin Smith, Adam Vroman,
Edward Curtis, Arnold Genthe and
Darius Kinsey

Praeger Publishers
New York · Washington

CONTENTS:

FOREWORD:

Old photographs do various things for us but one of their main functions is to offer, in the aggregate, a broad cross-section of life at a certain period. The United States between 1880 and 1915 resembled a crazy quilt, composed of many races and ways of life. Most of America's 76 million people—the new immigrants and native Indian population, the New England farmers and black Southern sharecroppers—lived in relatively closed societies and had little awareness of different ways of life in other parts of America. Many Americans had never traveled more than a few miles from their birthplaces; each section maintained unique habits and traditions.

One photograph at the center of this book may be a touchstone for both the diversity of American life seventy years ago and the suggestive power of old photographs. The photographer Joseph Pennell leaned out of his window one October afternoon at the exact turn of the century, in the exact geographical center of the United States—Junction City, Kansas—and took a picture of his street (illustration 78). Pennell's photograph, dated by him as "1900," recorded what many of us think of as the core of American life in those days: Main Street in a small town, farm wagons and horses, cheerful bustle on the sidewalks, and a courthouse tower in the background. If we look at the photograph only in terms of the year it was taken, however, it tends to confirm our preconceptions about the past. We should think of the picture as preserving a single moment in a single place, rather than symbolizing a year or an era. In the center of the photograph there is a wagon, loaded with building blocks, turning into an alley. If we place ourselves at the moment the photograph was taken, we can use the wagon's turning the corner as a reference point from which to look at other, simultaneous moments all across the United States. We then realize that almost any of the other photographs in this book could have been taken at the instant the wagon pulled off Main Street, and we see that Pennell's photograph represents only one type of life being lived at that moment.

Junction City, in any case, was not altogether typical. Only 60 percent of the population lived in small towns in 1900. As the wagon turned into the alley, there were two million children toiling in the mines and mills of the East, and 500,000 immigrants crowded into a few square blocks on New York's Lower East Side. While Pennell took his photograph, an old farm woman in Maine walked back and forth at her spinning wheel, just as her mother and grandmother had before her (illustration 3); in Washington State, six lumberjacks jostled into the cut of a giant tree to pose for a man in a derby hat (illustration 140). One of the book's portfolios shows us black sharecroppers who were still living in the same conditions they had endured under slavery; their children were being brought into the lifestyle of white America at Tuskegee Institute while the citizens of Junction City did their afternoon shopping. Vacationers at the Wisconsin Dells knew nothing about the round of extravagant entertainment engaged in by New York Society people: and New York Society had never been to a church social such as excited the inhabitants of Junction City. One can take almost any of these portfolios and use it, not as a rose-lensed telescope for looking back into the past, but as a place to stand, within the past, and look across the complex expanse of the whole country.

The various ways of life, while stable in themselves, were caught in shifts and changes. The American nation was on the move, and often one group would elbow another out—as the white settlers did to the Indians. A tremendous growth of industry after the Civil War had created new living habits as well as new jobs for people. With the first photograph in this book, one can see the contrast between the unprofitable New England farms and the flourishing New England mills. The photographs of New York City juxtapose the old landed gentry with the poor and the very rich—both products of the new industrial surge. We now know that the crazy quilt of America in 1900 would be torn apart in World War I, and that the new communication lines of the 1920's—the radio, the movies and the car—would stitch it together so closely that the seams would virtually disappear. Today American society is far more homogeneous than ever before; we watch the same television programs, have access to the same films, own the same automobiles, and are concerned about the same crises.

Some of the photographers who are represented in this book were professional, some were amateur, almost all were obscure. Up to now their work has been published, if at all, as single pictures plucked from the collections to make some particular point. We have kept each person's work in its own portfolio because we feel that there is both a valuable unity of subject and an aesthetic unity in any one photographer's study of a particular way of life.

We know that the camera captures moments that change before the photographer folds his equipment and leaves the scene. These photographers captured, at the last moment of stability, pieces of a world that was about to vanish. Their pictures are a map of the territory we have just covered, and perhaps if we read them carefully we will gain a clearer understanding of where we are now.

THE WAY LIFE WAS

CHANSONETTA EMMONS:

There were 3318 deserted farms in the state of Maine in 1890. For three generations the young people had been leaving the rocky, used-up fields to go West. The small local ports—where clipper ships had offered an alternative way of life to farm work—decayed as shipping was routed to cities where the railroads came in from the West. North of Boston, rural life preserved old ways in quiet backwaters. Like the rest of the United States, northern New England in the 1890's was shifting from an agrarian to an industrial economy; and as industrial energy drew more and more people to the cities, Maine became farther and farther "down east." Even the mills that mushroomed in the river valleys of Massachusetts, Rhode Island and Connecticut were never built in the states more remote from the centers of trade. An old sea captain in one of Sarah Orne Jewett's Maine stories from that period says, "I view it . . . that a community narrows down and grows dreadfully ignorant when it is shut up to its own affairs and gets no knowledge of the outside world . . . I call it low-water mark now here in Dunnet." Kingfield, Maine, where Chansonetta Stanley Emmons (1858–1937) was born, lay "up country" near the Canadian border. The village had 800 people in 1900, most of them descendants of the town's founder, "Squire" Solomon Stanley, who built the first frame house in town in 1812. There was a local saying that if you threw an apple in Kingfield, you were sure to hit a Stanley. Chansonetta was the only daughter among six children. Her twin brothers, F. E. and F. O. Stanley, developed a dry-plate photography process in the 1880's and became famous in the late 1890's with their invention of the Stanley Steamer automobile. In 1887 Chansonetta had married James Emmons, who ran a shoestore in Roxbury, Massachusetts. It was after his death in 1898 that she became seriously interested in photography. She returned to Kingfield to the family home every summer and, armed with her twin brothers' dry plates, she began to record the antique ways of her family connection and their friends.

The industry of Kingfield was restricted to country necessities made in mills that were run by the Carabassett River's water power. They produced wheelbarrow handles, wooden rakes, wagon poles, sap buckets and, in one building, axe handles. In the countryside, farm life was as exacting as it had always been and it had none of the possibilities of reward that farming the rich soil of the West offered. The day started at 5 a.m. in summer, 6 a.m. in winter; there were chores to be done before breakfast, and the day didn't end until you slipped between sheets, woven at home and laundered with homemade soap, shortly after sundown.

Chansonetta Emmons' notes on her negative cases make the daily life sound more

WAY DOWN EAST

attractive to us than it probably was. These old women working in the kitchens were
called Hannah and Abigail and Aunt Lucy Carville; the men were called Emery
and Warren and Tristram. At haying time they refreshed themselves in the field with a
swig of cool raspberry or blackberry shrub, and the white clapboard houses were
shaded by elms and hidden behind lilac bushes.

When visiting the remote farms she photographed, Chansonetta Emmons would develop
the negative plates at night in open pans, with blankets pinned to the windows and the
room lighted by a candle with a ruby glass shade. She had done portrait miniatures
in oil for years before she began to photograph; and, despite makeshift work
conditions, she achieved a painter's subtlety with composition and lighting. She
employed a flood of light behind her subject deliberately, as a reminiscence of
Rembrandt's use of backlighting. Although she made photographs off and on until her
death in 1937, the period of her greatest productivity was the late 1890's and early
1900's. Chansonetta Emmons applied a painter's eye to her camera and captured a
culture preserved as perfectly as a fly in amber.

Her people are the heirs of the Puritan farmers who left England in the 17th century,
determined to cleanse their lives of any business that did not relate to the glory of God.
By the 1890's no one was left on New England farms but old people—and
children who would leave as soon as they were big enough. But spareness was a quality
that New Englanders had originally sought in life. As the historian and critic Van
Wyck Brooks put it, now that old women alone in remote villages were so poor that they
had to make do with "a boiled potato and jelly for supper, saving their one egg for
breakfast," the fine bones beneath the body of New England life were revealed.

1.

Maine farm children, when they weren't doing chores such as milking or chopping wood or hauling water, were dressed up and sent to school. Education always played an important part in New England life for even the humblest citizens.

2.

Haymaking had to be done, as everyone knows, while the sun was shining, because if wet hay was put in the barn spontaneous combustion might result. Stacking the slippery hay onto a "wain"—or wagon—so that it didn't fall off was an exacting and precise process. Many a hired man, who had little else to be proud of in a lifetime of toil, preened himself on his skill at building a stack.

3.

Spinning was one of the home crafts, outmoded in a newly mechanized United States, that lingered on in the remote parts of New England, where old women maintained the ways their families had lived for generations. The large spinning wheel was a flax wheel. Flax was spun stepping back and forth between the wheel and the spindle, and women sometimes walked miles a day doing their spinning. The room where the old lady works is a jumble of homemade and mass-produced furnishings. One chair has a cover of factory-made calico; the other was probably made, and its seat caned, at home. The rag rug was braided at home from scraps of worn-out clothes, the fine panels in the doors were most likely fashioned by a country carpenter. On the other hand, the wallpaper comes from a Sears, Roebuck catalogue.

4.

Mrs. Emmons photographed Emery Butts sitting in a table-chair, an heirloom reputed to have come down from the 1600's. The table-chair is in the well shed, one of the outhouses that connected a New England farmhouse with the barn and enabled a farmer to get his animals without going out in the snow. The well, with its wooden cover and rope, is on Mr. Butts' left.

5.

Winter was the off-season on a farm, and there was leisure to sit in the blacksmith shop in New Portland, Maine, around the heat of the forge. One man reads the local newspaper, the only source of outside information for the village other than personal letters; and the other man, whose name was Warren Swett, quietly regards the photographer and her work. A row of ready-made horseshoes hangs across the window.

6.

Chansonetta Emmons photographed her daughter, Dorothy, surrounded by pursuits suitable to a well-bred young lady. She has an amply pillowed window seat where she can read The Ladies' Home Journal *or* The Youth's Companion, *and the Venus de Milo graces the piano with her ideal body. The piano was a status symbol and an important source of entertainment before movies and the radio.*

7.

The pace of country life, leisurely at best, had slowed down to an amble in the years before World War I. When Dorothy Emmons was photographed by her mother in the summer of 1910, it seemed as though she might always have sat on a rock, in her middy blouse, waiting for the tide to come in.

FRANCES BENJAMIN JOHNSTON:

In 1821, the officers of the Boston Manufacturing Company Textile Mills, which had been founded by a Bostonian with the invincibly aristocratic name of Francis Cabot Lowell, built a new factory at the junction of the Concord and Merrimack rivers in Massachusetts. Within 15 years, so many other factories had been erected that a new town was incorporated and named Lowell. Its population had exploded from 200 to 17,000. One of the reasons for this mushrooming of industry was, of course, the introduction of English weaving machinery into New England at the turn of the 19th century. Another reason, however, was the mill-owners' discovery that a great untapped work force existed in the single women of rural Massachusetts, New Hampshire and Vermont.

The idea of a permanent proletariat, pasty-faced and underfed, tied to machinery, always loomed as a great evil in the early years of the republic. So there was great delight at what seemed a solution to this exploitation when the mill-owners hit on the idea of company-owned boarding houses, strictly chaperoned, where virtuous country girls could stay while they worked for a few years, accumulating a dowry or helping to support their families. Model mill towns, approaching the utopian, grew up around Lowell and maintained their character well into the 1850's. The work force constantly shifted as girls went home to get married and new ones came into town.

After 1850, the influx of poverty-stricken Irish into New England and the increasing greed of the mill-owners, who assigned more work to the girls and cut wages rather than dividends, began to create just the proletariat that the original mill-owners wanted to avoid. But a dignity had been given to working women that could not be erased. Before the mills offered them employment they had no choice but to be dependent at home or teach school for a term or two. Long after 1895, when Frances Benjamin Johnston (1864–1952) photographed the women shoe-workers of Lynn, Massachusetts, New England's airy brick and wood factory buildings and well-built company-owned homes gave self-respect as well as jobs to widows and single girls.

Frances Benjamin Johnston was in one way a very appropriate person to document the lives of the women workers of Lynn. Many of the photographers in this book took pictures of their home environment or went out to study a milieu with which they were already bound up emotionally or artistically. But Frances Johnston searched out assignments as a professional reporter. One of the first photojournalists who created news stories in pictures, she supported herself by her own efforts.

She was born in Grafton, West Virginia, and trained as an artist at the Académie

WOMEN IN THE MILL

Julien in Paris. She returned to Washington, D.C., and fell into the life of a well-to-do young dilettante. Late in the 1880's a friend, who served as Washington correspondent for a New York paper, asked Frances to take over her job while she was out of town for a while. Frances agreed and thought the paper would more readily accept the interviews she did if they were accompanied by photographs of the subjects. So she wrote to another newcomer in the photography field, George Eastman, who had marketed the Kodak rollfilm in 1888, the year before. "Please send me a camera which will take good pictures for newspapers," she said.

In addition to the camera, which worked well, she was blessed with impeccable social connections and a cool, orderly eye. Her photography career was launched. During the 1890's she began to do picture stories for magazines, including an innovative photo essay on the coal fields of Pennsylvania and a series of pictures of Admiral Dewey's "Great White Fleet," which was returning triumphant from the Spanish-American War. It was in 1895 that Frances Johnston went to the shoe mills of Lowell.

Although she was aware of the social impact of her photographs, Frances Johnston thought of her camera as a way of making interpretive works of art, not social documents. In the 1930's the American Institute of Architects commissioned her to do a "photographic record of the early architecture of the nine southern states, from Maryland to Florida." This work has been called her "greatest glory." That judgment is debatable, but her enthusiasm for architecture was related to her interest, as a photographer, in order, patterns and compositions.

The photographs she took at Lowell are carefully composed to reveal the quiet pride in the faces of the working women. The photographs reflect not only the way mill life was lived in a certain Massachusetts town in 1895, but an ideal about the dignity of labor everywhere.

9

8.

The mills were usually built beside a canal or river so that water power could be harnessed to run the machines. The proximity of workers' homes to the mill represented the first attempts at urban planning in the United States.

9–10.

The New England poet John Greenleaf Whittier called the women factory workers "fair unveiled Nuns of Industry." These women probably did not regard putting glue on shoe soles as a vocation, but there is certainly a serenity and sense of self-respect in their faces, rare to factory workers. The young worker's brooch and the supervisor's gold watch were sources of pleasure to their owners, but they are not worn as though they were exceptional. The women's pay was approximately ten or twelve dollars a week for a twelve-hour day.

11.

The mills usually closed down at 7 p.m. with the workers having started the day, like farmers, at 5 a.m. The girls and the lone male bookkeeper leave for an evening in which they may still have the energy to visit, or dance, or even read. The awnings, the girl's flowered hats and the parasol add a note of summer gaiety.

12.

The English traveler Harriet Martineau noted in 1835 that the boot- and shoe-makers of Lynn took time off in the summer to go fishing. Mill town life had tightened up when Frances Johnston photographed the children of the workers playing ring-around-the-rosy in 1895. But the mill-owned apartments are still a far cry from the workers' tenements in other parts of the country.

ALICE AUSTEN:

In 1866 the Civil War was just over. New York City, with a population of 900,000, was still a middle-sized port city with a provincial aristocracy composed of old Dutch and English families. They had owned land and traded there since the Dutch bought Manhattan from the Indians. Until the 1840's aristocratic control of the Hudson Valley was such that the heirs of the Dutch patroon families even had the feudal right to condemn tenants of their land to death. The industrial fortunes of the 1870's had not yet created the Goulds and Vanderbilts and the "400" leaders of Society; and in old New York everyone of the leading families still knew, and was related to, everyone else. It was "The Age of Innocence" written about by Edith Wharton, who said "the world of fashion was still content to reassemble every winter in the shabby red and gold boxes of the sociable old Academy of Music. Conservatives cherished it for being small and inconvenient, and thus keeping out the 'new people' whom New York was beginning to dread and yet be drawn to."

Staten Island, where Alice Austen (1866–1952) was born into this old aristocracy, was a pastoral haven in New York Harbor. The Austen home, named Clear Comfort, had been built before 1700. Alice's grandfather and great-grandfather were prosperous dry-goods auctioneers, a very respectable occupation in a city that lived by trade. One of the treasured family curios was some massive links of a chain forged by Alice's great-great-grandfather, Peter Townsend, which had been stretched across the Hudson in 1778 to keep the British from sailing up the river and capturing Benedict Arnold's army at West Point.

When she was ten years old, an uncle who was a sea captain let Alice use his camera. Another uncle taught her about photographic chemicals, and for the next fifty years she took pictures—over 7000 of them—almost all on glass-plate negatives, which she washed under the kitchen pump. She was a meticulous craftswoman, and on the envelopes of all her negatives she noted the time of day, the light conditions and the shutter speed she had used.

What she photographed was the life around her, the life of a genteel young lady, a life she later described as "larky." She attended Errington School for Young Ladies and the Staten Island Garden Club. She won prizes at golf and tennis; and she often accompanied her mother on long country visits to houses where the big event was staying up all night in the parlor to watch the night-blooming cereus put out its once-in-a-decade blossom. There were balls at Christmas time, and masquerade parties and fox hunting across farmers' fields in the fall. Every summer the Austens and various friends repaired to a cabin on Lake Mahopac, just north of New York City.

VICTORIAN GENTRY

Alice does not seem to have had any particular beau—a grave dilemma since the main business of an upper class young girl was to get married—but she always had an escort; and people went places in groups in those days, which camouflaged a girl's single state. Underneath the frivolity, however, the support of this life was tradition, which set both a precedent and a standard for every action. The only acceptable behavior was in familiar patterns. The stiff poses of the subjects in many of Alice Austen's photographs contrast with the human moment in the photograph of "Norman Nichols and Miss?" where the participants seem to have been surprised in an intimate conversation.

After the turn of the century, Alice, defined as an old maid as she entered her thirties, took fewer photographs. By the time of World War I, when Staten Island had become a suburb of New York, she ceased using her camera almost entirely. In middle age Alice lived more and more in retirement at Clear Comfort with Gertrude Tate, an old friend. In 1929, when the stock market collapsed, Alice's capital was washed away. First she mortgaged Clear Comfort, then she sold the furniture and curios bit by bit. Finally the bank foreclosed, but let her live on as caretaker. She and Gertrude tried to open a restaurant in the house, but they didn't know how to pare down the portions of steak and lobster and chicken, and Alice couldn't bring herself to serve liquor in the family home, so the venture failed. The bank sold Clear Comfort for $7500. After a series of makeshift homes, Alice, crippled and in a wheelchair, finally went to the Staten Island Poorhouse in 1950.

Then the Staten Island Historical Society discovered her photographs. She was published in *Life* and she spent the last months before her death in 1952 in a private nursing home. Clear Comfort is still standing, battered and shabby, but Alice Austen's world, ordered, serene and sure, has disappeared with its people.

13.

*On Staten Island in the late 1890's things were generally
serene, and every season had its appointed pleasure:
tennis in the spring and summer, hunting in the winter,
and to fill the long summer days—visits.*

14.

Two horses to a light carriage were an extravagance, for only one was necessary. The vehicle used for paying calls in summer was a dogcart; it required a coachman and horses with cropped tails to keep up the good name of the family.

15.

Tennis was first introduced to the United States from Bermuda at the Staten Island Cricket and Baseball Club in 1874, not far from Alice Austen's home. In 1888 Alice and her friend, Trude Eccleston, the rector's daughter, went to play with the officers at Fort Wadsworth. On Staten Island the game apparently involved more decorum than activity.

16

16.

At 5:15 on Friday, June 7, 1895, the sun cast long shadows across the turf of the Ladies' Club. The lawn tennis nets were up, young gentlemen guests held tight to favorite racquets and tea was being served under a marquee.

17.

In 1910 the Austen family car was a Peerless, resplendent with four visible cylinders and a rimless spare tire on the opposite running board.

18.

One of Alice's "larks" was posing with Trude Eccleston, both of them got up as "fast women." They arranged curtains to suggest a stage, a dubious setting in itself,

wore only their corsets and short petticoats, and "smoked" rolled up pieces of paper. Their hair was down (as improper in grown women as it was correct for young girls) and, to assure anonymity (also bad in a society where everyone knew everyone else), they wore masks.

19.

Alice photographed a group of summer neighbors at Lake Mahopac one afternoon in 1888.

18

17

20

20.

In 1890 there was still enough open country on Staten Island to ride horses across it on a fox hunt. The idea was an English import that appealed to American gentry. The two people who seem to be caught in a tryst were at a hunt breakfast; the photographer's caption remembered the dapper man, whose name was Norman Nichols, but dismissed the veiled lady as "Miss ?"

21.

A favorite Austen family excursion was up the Hudson to Fishkill, a home of the van Rensselaers, an old Dutch patroon family. The van Rensselaers had received a land grant of 20 miles along the Hudson River from the Dutch government in 1629. They ruled autocratically; and a vestige of their glory remained when Alice photographed Mrs. Austen and Mrs. Rusten van Rensselaer ("Mama and Cousin Jane") on the piazza one summer morning in a frame of pillars, clapboarding and shutters.

JACOB RIIS:

One Saturday in the 1880's a small boy on New York's Lower East Side spent the day
carrying buckets of beer to workingmen, one of whom was his father. He was
probably less than ten years old or he himself would have been working. By the end
of the day, exhausted and undernourished, the boy was drunk enough from sips of beer
to go down into the cellar of the workshop and fall into a stupor. He didn't
return home to his family's tenement flat on Sunday. On Monday morning when the
shop was opened, he was found in the cellar, killed by rats and half eaten.
This story was one Jacob August Riis (1849–1914), police reporter, social reformer and
photographer, wrote up in the *Evening Sun*. Riis's interest in the immigrant slums
that festered in lower Manhattan began with his own experience as a homeless
immigrant. Born in Ribe, Denmark, in 1849, the son of the town schoolmaster,
he was apprenticed to a carpenter, but he left for America when his proposal
of marriage was turned down by a rich mill-owner's golden-haired daughter. He landed
at Castle Garden, New York's immigrant reception center, in 1870 and for
the next three years he worked in Pennsylvania, upstate New York and New York City
as a mill hand and a traveling salesman. At times he was reduced to chopping
some farmer's wood in order to get a meal. When he was finally hired by the New York
News Association, he fainted from hunger after his first day.
Newspaper work, however, was the perfect outlet for Riis's energetic indignation
at the poverty he encountered; and in 1877 (after a trip back to Denmark to marry the
mill-owner's daughter) he became a police reporter working out of Mulberry
Street in what he called "the foul core of New York's slums." There tenements
housed as many as 276,000 people to the square mile, with more coming every
year. Germans, Irish, Chinese, Italians and Eastern European Jews all suffered in
their own thronged enclaves. There 155 children under five years of age died in one block
in one year, and a piece of bread and a pickle was considered a good supper.
The total income for a family might be $2.70 per week, with the rent on two squalid,
airless rooms as much as $7.00 per month. Children of twelve or thirteen were
paid $2\frac{1}{2}$¢ per hour for sewing work in "sweatshops"—apartments where whole families
did handwork. To pay the rent most families took in "boarders," so that as many
as ten or twelve people slept in one room. Space, light and air were as hard to come by
as food and clothing. Babies were asphyxiated by the very air of their homes;
on the first hot night in June police dispatches were filled with reports of sleepers
rolling off window sills and roofs, where they had tried to catch enough air to
breathe.

HOW THE OTHER HALF LIVED

Riis's lively journalistic sense and his yearning to communicate the horrors he saw attracted him to the camera early in his career. He taught himself to take pictures, but he was clumsy and twice set fire to rooms where he was using flash powder.

The photographs that he finally achieved have unparalleled graphic power. They add details of poverty that even his naive, forceful prose cannot convey. For Riis, the root of slum misery was the tenement's lack of space and privacy; and his harsh photographs are as crowded as the life there itself. There was no room for the photographer to step back from his subjects, and they confront him directly, sharing a brutal, rank intimacy.

Because no engraving process at that time was sophisticated enough to reproduce them in a newspaper, Riis converted his pictures to "magic lantern" slides and showed them around the country at fund-raising meetings and to reform groups.

His shows were so successful that he was asked to expand a magazine article, "How the Other Half Lives," into a book. Again the photographs had to be copied as drawings but the book's publication in 1890 initiated the most influential period of his career. Before 1903 he wrote four more books about life in the slums and his work there, including his autobiography, *The Making of an American*.

Theodore Roosevelt, whom Riis knew when Roosevelt was President of the New York City Board of Police Commissioners, called him "the most useful citizen of New York." Riis's view of the slums was basically that of a European: he felt that these poor souls were caught in a static class structure which would never offer them an alternative to their degradation—and that something had to be done to make their lot bearable. Looking at Riis's photographs, it is easy to appreciate his feeling that the poor were caught in a permanent struggle for subsistence. In retrospect, we know that then the United States was a still-expanding country that needed manpower, and the children of immigrants did get jobs and follow a fairly broad path out of the Lower East Side; and despite his pessimism about effecting lasting change, it was Riis's efforts that helped America's newest citizens take the first step off the treadmill.

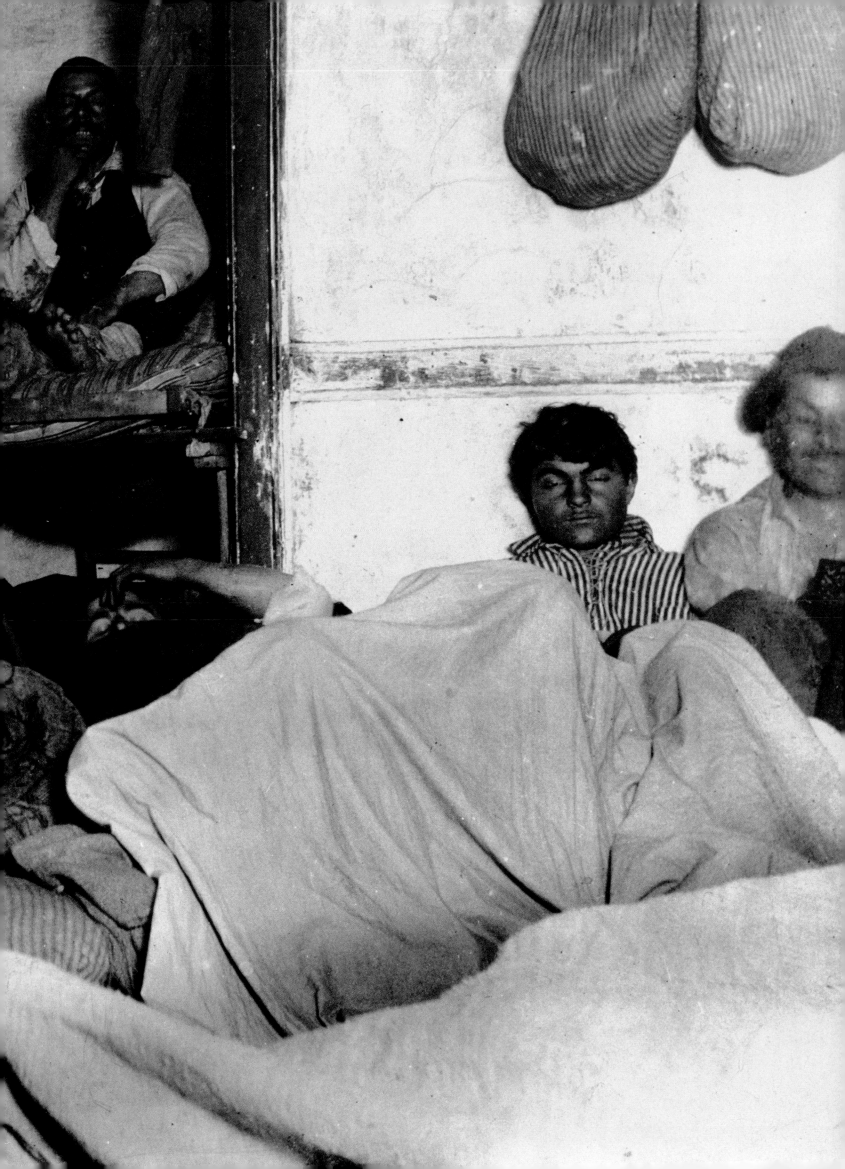

27.

*"Five-cents-a-spot" lodgings, although they were illegal,
flourished for the immigrants who had no families. Riis
described this one:*

*"In a room not thirteen feet either way slept twelve
men and women, two or three in bunks set in a sort of
alcove, the rest on the floor. A kerosene lamp
burned dimly in the fearful atmosphere, probably to guide
other and later arrivals to their 'beds,' for it was
just past midnight."*

28.

*At the beginning of a lifelong struggle children played in
Mullen's Alley near Mulberry Street. Riis called this
area the "foul core of New York's slums." With filthy
lanes six feet wide as their only playground, the
children died at the rate of 155 in a block per year.*

29.

*The law for children working in New York was ten hours
a day, no one under sixteen unless he could read
English and no one under fourteen at all. But ten- and
twelve-year-olds often swore they were of age and no
one bothered to find out to the contrary. Work at such
an age was self-defeating because it eliminated school—
the only avenue out of the slums. Education such
as the 52nd Street Industrial School offered was minimal
and entailed severe sacrifices for the family, who not
only had to do without their child's income, but were
obliged as well to clothe him properly for school.*

LEWIS HINE:

In 1905 children ten and eleven years old worked in the anthracite coal mines in eastern Pennsylvania. Many of the boys worked in the "breakers," which meant that they sat on wooden boards over a chute which tons of coal rattled through; they bent over and picked out the stone and slate from the good coal. A ten-year-old doing this ten hours a day became very fatigued, developed round shoulders, and his growth was stunted, but those long-term effects were not the worst dangers. The threat hanging over the boys was that if one lost his balance and fell off the board into the chute, he would be crushed by the new loads of coal crashing down the chute.

All around the Southern coast, oyster and shrimp canneries, in the same years, employed children to open the oysters and clean the shrimp. The shells on the oysters cut tiny fingers brutally and the children got a nickel for a four-pound pail of oyster meat; they could fill one or two pails a day. The shrimp were worse than the oysters because they secreted a thick liquid, like lye, which ate holes in the tin buckets and the children's shoes. When their hands bled too badly to work they soaked them in an alum solution to harden the skin.

Lewis Hine (1874–1940) was a young photographer hired by the National Child Labor Committee to document these abuses—abuses that were defended by factory- and mill-owners as benefiting the nation generally and the child employees specifically. The jobs, they claimed, would turn the children into responsible adults who could keep themselves. In fact, child labor turned those who reached adulthood into maimed, stunted slaves with no reserves of bodily strength or sense of responsibility to the community that had exploited them. There were no effective state or government controls over children working. In many states, although fourteen was the minimum age for employment, no proof was required, and because there was no limit on hours, ten-year-old children were working twelve- and fourteen-hour days. Concern about this situation among ministers, educators and social workers had led to the organization of the National Child Labor Committee on April 15, 1904. The Committee favored federal legislation on child labor and caught the ear of President Theodore Roosevelt, who cabled: "Come down and tell me about it."

In 1908, as an aid in getting legislation through Congress, the Committee hired Hine, who had experience in the mills himself. When he was fifteen, he had gone to work in a furniture factory in the lumber town of Oshkosh, Wisconsin, where he was born. He had to walk for a mile to work, in winter over a frozen river, to the shop where he was paid $4 a week for six fifteen-hour days. He managed to get an education, however, and his first job after college was as a nature teacher at the School for Ethical

CHILDREN IN BONDAGE

Culture in New York. He began to photograph in 1903. After receiving a sociology degree from Columbia University in 1905, he did extensive work with the immigrants at Ellis Island, New York City. He resigned his teaching job when the National Child Labor Committee hired him. He worked off and on for them and for magazines and foundations for the rest of his life. Hine's pictures of immigrants and children in the mills were printed and made into stereopticon slides and used in lectures all over the country.

When Hine began to take photographs, the Child Labor Committee relied on the 1900 census figures that they knew were inaccurate, but even by those figures the child labor force had grown from 1,000,000 in 1870 to nearly 2,000,000 in 1900. Eighteen percent of the nation's children between ten and fifteen years old were employed. The hours they worked meant that they could seldom go to school; and, in parts of the South where most of the cotton mills were, poverty-stricken parents and brutal mill-owners argued that school was a waste of time anyway. Not only was an ignorant, culturally deprived proletariat growing up in the mills and mines, but the health of most mill children was wrecked by the ceaseless heavy labor extorted from growing bones and muscles. And yet, surprisingly, the children in Hine's photographs are particularly poignant just because they are not all wizened little automatons. Many of them are rather handsome children and they look with interest—and sometimes animation—at the photographer. The small miner whose shirt is torn and whose lip has a scab from a beating or an accident and the little girl who has turned her back on the throbbing rows of spindles for one glimpse out the window both seem to be looking at—or for—the possibility of another life.

The effect of the exploitation was far spread. Unlike the children, the adults don't respond to the photographer in any way—enthusiastically or wearily. Anything out of the daily grind is only a shock. The adults or youths who stand over the working children in supervision are dehumanized completely; they enjoy their power.

Hine's children were resilient. Even after some years at work they could be rescued, and they would still constitute the nation's greatest resource. If they were not rescued they turned into the soulless drudges or vicious exploiters who stand in these photographs with them.

43

44

43–44.

The mills often maimed children physically, and the damage done to their minds was as bad as the abuse of their bodies. They sometimes grew up to enjoy a modicum of power when they could abuse young workers as they had been. The lint-covered cotton mill children are supervised in Hine's photographs by adolescents who seem cruel and arrogant and an adult who looks like Simon Legree. No employee had a life out from under mill control. Whole Southern villages were owned by the mills—church, school, store, cemetery and doctor, as well as the houses.

45.

Working on the street as messengers and newsboys wasn't as physically debilitating as mill and mine work, but in other ways it was the worst of all for children. Messengers like the cocky young man with his cap, pipe and bicycle were often used to carry notes to brothels where the inmates "tipped" them with their usual services. Accustomed to working at all hours with little supervision, messengers frequently were unable to hold more structured jobs as adults.

46.

There was no regulation of street trades before 1902, and many newsboys were as young as six and eight years old. The child bought the papers from the dealer and lost money on any he didn't sell.

HENRY HAMILTON BENNETT:

A St. Louis newspaper of the 1880's described an area of rocky gorges and islets on the Wisconsin River, called the Wisconsin Dells, as "a wondrous, witch-like tangle of cliffs, crags, caverns and gulches, of strange-shaped towering rocks, yawning chasms and roaring floods, all decked out with ferns and flowers and cataract foam, all filled with the music of falling waters and winds sweeping through dark and labyrinthian halls." There was a new leisure in American life in those days, and a romantic area like the Dells had great appeal. For the first time people had time enough, at least in the settled land east of the Mississippi, to indulge in pursuits other than the struggle for survival. Those who had moved to the city to work in the industries that sprang up after the Civil War now began to take vacations and they usually wanted to spend them in the country. At the Dells the Milwaukee citizen could disport himself in the pioneer tradition of man in a one-to-one confrontation with the wilderness, all the while keeping his top hat and umbrella.

The popularity of the Dells came about largely through the efforts of the local photographer, Henry Hamilton Bennett (1843–1908), who spent thirty years photographing and promoting the area. Bennett had been born in Canada and had gone to Wisconsin by way of Vermont when he was fourteen. Originally intending to be a carpenter, he had gone off to the Civil War and returned with a bullet in his hand, which forced him to change his occupation. He bought a tintype studio in Kilbourne City—soon to be renamed Wisconsin Dells—and photography was his work for the rest of his life. He left the lucrative portrait work to his wife and concentrated on landscape photography because, as he said, you didn't have to pose nature and it was less trouble to please than people.

Bennett was always clever with gadgets, and one of his first inventions was a homemade camera with which he could take stereoscope views of the landscape. (A stereoscope consisted of a wooden frame with two lenses; in front of these you put two nearly identical photographs, mounted side by side, and the result was a three-dimensional view.) Among his other innovations was the practice of placing soaked sponges next to his negative plates to keep them moist during the long exposure necessary while photographing inside the grottos and caves of the Dells.

Bennett's original way of photographing landscape brought rowboats and later excursion steamers full of straw-hatted and parasoled picnickers to the Dells. He was tireless in recording his paradise on glass plates. If there were grottos that the waterfalls made inaccessible in summer, he would wait until winter to photograph them, when he could clamber over the frozen water, the cumbersome camera equipment

WISCONSIN DELLS

of the period strapped to his back. He would return to the same spot time and again
over the forty years that he spent photographing the Dells, so that eventually
he had records of his favorite places in every kind of light and weather.
He hoped, always, to make other people see just the variety and wonder of the Dells that
he saw. It was Bennett's attitude as an early conservationist that encouraged
his children to purchase much of the Dells area and present it to the University
of Wisconsin as a means of preserving it.
Bennett was a nature poet with a camera, who could transfer his romantic image of the
landscape to the photographs he took. The frontier had moved past this
part of Wisconsin a generation earlier, and the nostalgia that people were already
beginning to feel for the wilderness coincided with Bennett's romantic
pictures. Vacations were a fresh idea to most Americans in those days, and Bennett
made the first and best vacation postcards. They presented what you wanted
to see when you went away—not necessarily what you got.

47.

After H. H. Bennett had publicized the Dells as a popular resort area, people went there in flotillas—of rowboats. Intrepid visitors, the ladies sheltered from the sun, used small boats if they planned to penetrate into the farthest grottos. Otherwise they did their sightseeing from a less maneuverable excursion steamer. "Native" guides in shirt sleeves rowed the boats.

48.

Bennett resented any industrial encroachment on his Dells, and wrote: "with me, every rock that is to be hidden from sight . . . is sacrilege of what God has done in carving them into beautiful shapes." The beautiful rocks often suggested domestic objects to the people naming them. Bennett photographed one man in front of "The Sugar Bowl."

49.

Bennett framed a tourist and his guide in the massive oval of the rocks at the entrance to "Boat Cave." The viewer has the impression of looking through a keyhole into a secret, idyllic world.

50.

The ruins of an old mill at "Pewitt's Nest" in the Baraboo Bluffs was a popular place to picnic. It is not a stage prop thunderbolt that hangs over the heads of Bennett's unsuspecting subjects but the remains of a mill wheel that some mechanical soul built in the natural sluice between the rocks.

50

51–52.
"Stand Rock" was one of the titillating hazards nature obligingly scattered about the Dells. Bennett did much experimenting with exposure time and shutter speeds. In 1887, he snapped a man's leap across the chasm using a shutter regulated with rubber bands. (*Ordinary shutter speeds would have blurred the image.*) Jumping the abyss was a test of nerve for an athletic, unfettered man. That ladies in cumbersome skirts managed it is remarkable enough; how they brought the picnic basket with them is a complete mystery.

53.
Bennett's landscapes resembled fashionable paintings of the period.

51

52

SOLOMON BUTCHER:

The artist and the dreamer always had a hard time in the frontier, where every man was expected to make his living by the sweat of his brow. And yet the frontier, like any culture, had its historians to record the life its people were building. Usually someone whom most people considered an idler wrote old settlers' memoirs or painted "primitive" scenes of a country's early days, and left for us the most vivid sense of what it was like to turn over forty acres of six-inch sod or cut down four trees a day. Those who, through lack of inclination or ability to do other work, had time to watch what was going on often had the deepest understanding of it after all. Solomon Butcher (1856–1927) was one of these people. He had failed as a salesman, a farmer and a medical student, when he conceived the idea of compiling his photographs as a history of the plains showing the transition from open prairie to breadbasket of America. The idea came to him in 1886, and he said, "From the time I thought of the history book, for seven days and nights it drove sleep from my eyes." This almost mystical vocation Butcher was to devote to the square miles of open, rolling prairie which the government mapmakers had designated Custer County, Nebraska. The effect of such vast areas of open land was described by Willa Cather in *My Antonia!:* "Everywhere, as far as the eye could reach, there was nothing but rough, shaggy, red grass, most of it as tall as I . . . the little trees were insignificant against the grass. It seemed as if the grass were about to run over them, and over plum-patch behind the sod chickenhouse.

"As I looked about me I felt that the grass was the country, as the water the sea. The red of the grass made all the great prairie the color of wine-stains, or of certain seaweeds when they are first washed up. And there was so much motion in it; the whole country seemed, somehow, to be running."

The grass had withered each fall and had sprung up richer every spring for millennia before the arrival of the settlers. The black prairie sod was the best earth in the world, and there were no stones such as littered the worn-out fields of the East, nor trees such as the farmers had had to clear on the Ohio and Wisconsin frontiers. But neither was there any wood to build a shelter. The U.S. government would freely deed a man 160 acres of flat farmland just for living on it for five years. But in what was he to live?

The answer for most of the earliest Nebraska settlers was the "soddy"—a house made of earth. The prairie turf, which the specially designed "grasshopper" plows turned over in strips from three to six inches thick, was matted with the grass roots into a mass the consistency of heavy rubber. These strips could be chopped into brick lengths and laid

SOD HOUSES

on one another to form walls. Pioneer wives complained about having to live in holes like animals, but actually the houses, for the most part raised above ground, endured in some cases for a hundred years. They provided marvelous insulation against the cold in winter and the heat in summer. Glass windows with wooden frames and door frames were added, as were board floors and whitewash, and only the roof was less than durable. The shortage of wood and canvas meant that the roof was usually sod laid across willow brush. At best, it bloomed with grasses and wild flowers in the summer; at worst, soggy with its own weight and not very waterproof anyway, it collapsed, covering the family inside in a mass of slimy mud.

The sod house was a testament to American resourcefulness and Butcher, moving around his county taking 1500 views of farmsteads and writing 1500 pioneers' biographies, recorded as well the tools and gadgets the pioneers contrived. His pictures are full of objects. Perhaps because the houses themselves are so much a part of the earth, lost in the waving grass, each photograph emphasizes possessions—playing cards, buggies, antlers crowning a well sweep. In one household all the family's domestic paraphernalia was dragged outside and placed squarely before the photographer as proof of achievement and, even more important in that trackless land, evidence of existence.

Butcher himself, driven by the same compulsion to make permanent and build something lasting in his county history, was set back in 1899 when his studio burned (it was wood; sod wouldn't have burned), taking all his written work. Fortunately his glass negatives were stored elsewhere and they survived. He rewrote many of the biographical details of his book and in the early 1900's an old cowman, Ephraim S. Finch, taken by Butcher's idea of chronicling the county, helped finance the publication of 1000 copies of the *Pioneer History of Custer County, Nebraska*. Butcher's aim had been accomplished. His real achievement, however, remains the photographic record of the primitive, solid people of his county, frozen in front of their soddys and their worldly goods.

54.

Many plains families first settled in a dugout: a cave dug out of a hillside with a fourth wall and a roof of mud. Pioneer wives regarded such homes as a shameful way to live and usually goaded their husbands to build above ground in a year or so. The people who posed with their cows have turned the dugout over to the animals; their new soddy, above ground, is one of the three inventions that made the treeless, waterless, unbounded plains habitable. The other two were the windmill, for drawing water from 300 and 400 foot deep wells, and barbed wire, for fencing in the animals. To get that apron white and the sunbonnet clean for the baby, the woman—living in a mud house—had to draw water, boil it, use precious

55

56

57

homemade soap, and then heat flatirons to press the clothes.

55–57.

Ingenious machines, typical of American know-how ever since Benjamin Franklin, made it easier to face the emptiness of the prairie and drudgery of sod-breaking. In 1889 C. Layton and his mother used a derrick to sink a 400 foot well on Cliff Table, Nebraska; in 1903 in Broken Bow a vast crowd attended the ascent of a balloon filled with helium.

Everything was on a grand scale on the prairie—the sky, the farms, even the ears of corn, and gadgets were no exception. The Brobdignagian toy below was a carpet cleaner: run by a gas engine, it tossed the carpets around the way a modern dryer tumbles clothes. It is not recorded whether it was an improvement over small boys who beat carpets on the clothesline at home.

58.

*There was a natural impulse to assert your individuality
in the vast silence of the plains. One possibly childless
couple posed their dog and horses and gathered
together their dearest possessions—sewing machine,
birds, plants and even a Christmas wreath—for the
photographer. The way the man holds his pitchfork
and the face of the woman bear a strong resemblance to
the farm couple in Grant Wood's* American Gothic,
painted forty years later.

59.

The only way to succeed in farming the arid plains was to let a portion of your fields lie uncultivated so they could store up moisture. The Perry brothers, dressed fit to kill in front of their bachelor soddy, seem to have devised ingenious ways to pass the time while their land lies fallow.

60.

The prairie had so few landmarks that a man could get lost in his own fields if the roof of his soddy blended into the grass. Without the soapbox, and the man and his team, little would distinguish this homestead from the roll of the plains.

59

60

L.W. HALBE:

Before the settlers arrived, the high central plains of Kansas were covered with a short tough grass that the early scouts and buffalo hunters called "buffalo grass." When the railroads pushed out from eastern Kansas in the late 1860's, the German, Irish and other immigrants who staked claims along the route of the tracks were not sure how to use this grass-covered land. It was much drier than any farm country they were accustomed to, and there were virtually no trees with which to build houses, barns or fences. Eventually, the windmill was succesfully employed to bring water up from wells hundreds of feet deep, barbed wire was invented for fences and the settlers discovered how to use the sod that their iron plows turned up as building blocks for sod houses. But there still was nothing that grew in the baking, dry summers and remorseless wind of the winters as well as buffalo grass. Then in 1873, members of a pacifist German religious sect called Mennonites, who had settled the steppes of Russia in the late 18th century, fled the czar's threat of compulsory military service and emigrated to Kansas. They brought with them a type of winter wheat (sown in the fall and harvested in the early summer) with hard red kernels that they had bred for the Russian plains. "Turkey red" wheat flourished in Kansas also, and at last there was a crop for the prairie.

Dorrance, Kansas, the town that L. W. Halbe (born c. 1895) photographed in the early years of the century, was a village of 281 citizens in 1910. It was totally dependent on the wheat farmers of the area, although its founding as a railroad town in the late 1860's antedated the introduction of "turkey red". Dorrance provided every service the farm families could not furnish for themselves: there was a school with 100 pupils and four teachers, four churches, a telephone operator, a Western Union telegraph office, a drugstore, a bank, a restaurant and, most important of all, the grain elevator and depot on the Union Pacific Railroad, where the wheat was shipped off to market. Farming, at the best of times, was precarious. Only when the crops were successful did the town prosper. In 1874 Kansas had been devastated by an army of locusts (grasshoppers). The legislature left a "Grasshopper Army" law on the books for fifty years whereby all the male citizens of a county over a certain age could be compelled to mobilize at the threat of another plague of insects. And there were less dramatic disasters of hail storms and drought. Farmers, who operated on a narrow cash margin, had to borrow money, often annually, because they needed extra horses at harvest time.

Life was demanding and would seem quite barren to us today. Dorrance had none of the Main Street diversions that a larger town, such as a county seat, would

PRAIRIE VILLAGE

provide. Kansas was technically a "dry" state after 1880, and only cities like Topeka dared defy the teetotalers and operate illegal saloons. Dorrance had a soda fountain in the drugstore and church activities, and there might be a sedate buggy ride for courting couples on Sunday afternoons, but, mostly, people worked. Indeed, the wheat farmers worked their three or four hundred acres so successfully that, by 1930, the topsoil was thoroughly pulverized. With no buffalo grass roots to hold it down, the land was eventually denuded by wind storms. The "dust bowl" was the result of that early industry.

The fall in Dorrance was the season for plowing and sowing the "turkey red" wheat; it was harvested in ten or twelve back-breaking days around the first of July. Other seasons brought the alfalfa harvest and hay mowing. One of the few pleasures heartily indulged in was eating the food you had raised, grown, or hunted and prepared yourself. The extent of this indulgence is indicated in a surviving Kansas Thanksgiving menu from the 1890's. It included: wild turkey soup, boiled wild turkey, roast venison and roast rabbit, rabbit pie and turkey giblets, broiled quail, home-canned tomatoes and lima beans and—strangely enough—"desiccated" potatoes, biscuits, rice pudding, pies and tarts.

L. W. Halbe, the photographer, was the banker's son in Dorrance. His father had moved there in the 1890's from New York City. Halbe—who later fought in France in World War I and became a member of the American Bar Association—when he was a young man wandered around town taking photographs of his friends and neighbors.

One Memorial Day—also called "Decoration Day" because that was when people decorated their family graves with flowers and wreaths—Halbe climbed to the top of the water tower, the only height near Dorrance, and photographed the whole town spread out before him. Dorrance was definitely a statement for civilization on the surface of the plains. But the villagers worked so hard on the land that they used it up, and, eventually were left with only dust.

61.
In August of 1908, the Union Pacific Depot in Dorrance,
Kansas, was a gateway to any place in the world.
Only, as the distances posted on the depot's side make
clear, it was a considerable ways before you arrived
any place.

62.
From the vantage point of the water tower on Decoration Day, 1911, Dorrance was raw and new looking, but it was not bleak. There was greenery and, as far as the eye could see, the prairie was cultivated. Nonetheless, the only thing in sight not completely practical is the fading circus poster on the side of the barn announcing a bygone parade on May 9.

63.
Rural Free Delivery of the United States mail was initiated by the postmaster general in 1896, relieving the isolation of remote farms. Three wagons went out daily from the Dorrance post office, combating blizzards, mud and dust. The photographer's caption called them "Uncle Sam's Boys."

64

65

64.

The bank was very important in Dorrance because of the narrow cash margin most farmers ran on. A rainstorm that ruined a hay crop could impoverish an otherwise self-sufficient family. The tellers' cages inspired awe concerning the mysteries of money, interest and the double-entry system of bookkeeping.

65.

The grain elevator was even more important than the railroad station. Gadabout people and luxuries came and went at the station, but crops were sent out from the elevator. Here the community corn-sheller is operating at the elevator, taking kernels off for meal and sending the cobs back home where they will be used for fuel.

66.

When settlers moved in, they always said the prairie was "opening up." In fact, the land was pinned down under a network of roads, the postal system and all the lines of communication. The telephone, the most modern, quickly became so important that the operator well deserved her title of "Central."

67.

There were four churches for Dorrance's 281 townspeople and families from the surrounding farms. The congregation of the Lutheran Church, some of them still wearing Old Country scarves, chatted around the sanctuary door one broiling Sunday in August.

68.

Sheetz's Restaurant, in a storefront on Main Street, served a family-style dinner at noon for 35¢. It is not known whether the cook always carried five cups in one hand or whether he was mugging, deadpan, for the camera.

69.

Jackson's Barber Shop, familiarly called "Jack's Tonsorial Parlor," had can-can girls on the wall and each customer's private shaving mug. On the prairie where everything was open to the best man and each acquisition dearly bought, the possession of his own shaving mug symbolized a man's standing as a respectable individual in the community.

70.

The photographs of the town all have a certain self-conscious tidiness, proper to civilization. The farm pictures, on the other hand, such as the one of a family on the water wagon spraying their crops, have an earthy reality that makes you sure the people were working before and after the picture. The family members are probably recent immigrants. The older families were snobbish about their women working in the fields: they said only peasants did that, and no American was a peasant.

69

JOSEPH PENNELL:

For the 45 million Americans who lived in villages of less than 2500 people at the turn of the century, the small-town store was the only civilization they knew. Sinclair Lewis says with irony in his 1920 novel, *Main Street,* that the Bon Ton Store represented the apogee of civilization. But digging a living from the resistant sod of the prairies allowed farmers little time for anything but life's necessities. The first towns on the prairie were never meant to be cultural centers; they merely served as depots on the railroad where farm produce was sent to market. Even the name of Junction City, Kansas, where J. J. Pennell (1866–1922) took his photographs, has a purely utilitarian ring: it lay at the junction of the Republican and Smoky Hill rivers (whose names, in turn, indicate no more than the county's political preference and its outstanding landmark). Practical as the settlers were, however, the human urge to decorate the most rigorous lives seems to be unquenchable; and by the time of Pennell's photographs, 30 years after its founding, Junction City was clothed in the latest gingerbread and curlicues. The main street offered saloons, cigars and bicycles as well as grain elevators and hardware stores.

The town was the meeting place for a wide section of the surrounding countryside, and it provided a variety of services. There were twenty restaurants, from sheds with a single table for all the customers—where you could get dinner for a quarter—to Frey's New Café, which served channel catfish or roast pork and apple sauce, à la carte, with pickled beets and, for dessert, raspberries and cream. The whole meal was laid on linen tablecloths and probably came to the extravagant sum of 55¢ or 60¢. In the drugstore you could get Wine of Cardui for one dollar and St. Jacob's Oil as well as the more prosaic Bromo Seltzer and wart remover for 10¢. Beef in the meat market was 10¢ a pound but breakfast bacon—expensive even then—was $12\frac{1}{2}$¢ per pound, and a 42-piece dinner set in the department store cost $2.95. And there were possibilities for folly—the grocery store offered canned green turtle meat for $2.75 a can. The average income for a 60-hour work week in 1900 was $12.74.

Joseph Pennell (no relation to the graphic artist and engraver of the same name who was his contemporary) had moved from North Carolina to Junction City with his parents when he was quite young. The contrast between the hilly, tired-out mountain farms of King's Creek and the empty, green prairie must have been considerable. By the time he was in his twenties Pennell began his professional photography career and was involved enough in his town to make a record of almost every detail of Junction City life. Pennell would stay in his office, doing the

PRAIRIE TOWN

portraits that provided his income: engaged couples, golden weddings, girl
graduates in white frocks, and suitors in celluloid collars, until something as picturesque
as an immigrant fruitseller or a man in a derby riding a bicycle went by, when he
would dash out and photograph it. We know, from the sparse records left,
that Pennell was a substantial citizen. He was a member of the Chamber of Commerce
for Junction City and the Rotary Club. Before his death at the age of 56 he had
received awards for his photographic work.

The enormous volume of his work came about because Pennell was an artist, with an
artist's compulsion to practice his craft incessantly, for love if not money. Junction City
would have been satisfied with studio portraits and the snapshots from
citizens' Brownies. But Pennell chronicled the town's life ceaselessly. There was a lot
to record, for what Junction City lacked in aesthetic interests, it made up for
in activity. No citizen of Junction City, or any Midwestern small town, was idle for a
moment in those days. There were few, if any, traveling theater companies and,
of course, no moving pictures for people to sit in front of and be entertained. As the
phrase went, they "made their own fun." Once or twice a month there were
literary societies like the Browning Society or the Thanatopsis Group; in the spring and
summer semi-professional baseball teams offered activity for any man, no
matter how he earned his living; there were sewing circles and several Methodist,
Presbyterian, Lutheran and Baptist churches that provided—in addition to prestige and
salvation—Sunday evening services (an occasion for courting), Wednesday
evening prayer meeting, Thursday evening choir practice, and often a social on Friday
night. Saturday night lodge groups had dances, and for the bibulous the saloons
always provided beer along with the cards.

The hours people in town worked—sixty per week—seem long today, although these
hours were insignificant beside the consuming labor of a farm. But the work
time did not begin to contain the overflowing energy of these people, who could build a
town where there had been only waving grass, make fun as well as a living for
themselves, and face the camera with the pride of their achievement. The Bon Ton
Store indeed represented the apogee of civilization.

71–74.
*Sports, saloons and cigars: the American small town had
come a long way from the 1630's, when the settlers
of Merrymount were driven out of Puritan Massachusetts
because they sang and danced around a Maypole.
Junction City, Kansas, offered baseball on Saturday
afternoons, with Zeek Guddy riding around town on a
ribbon-decked horse to announce the game; your
own shaving mug and a quarter haircut in Rudy Sahn's
barbershop; beer in the Horseshoe Saloon, because
Kansas had introduced Prohibition in 1880 and there
was nothing stronger; and any brand of cigar or chewing
tobacco in John Gartner's Cigar Store. Women were
not allowed in any of these male haunts; and none*

but Carry Nation, the fanatical anti-saloon crusader, would have wanted admittance. Feminine amusements in town involved the paying of calls, sewing circles, church groups and literary and amateur theatrical societies.

75

76

75–77.

1900 was a transition period for transportation. There were less than 150 miles of paved roads in the United States, and 8000 automobiles for a population of 76 million people. Long-distance trips, a rare event for most families, were made by train; otherwise people were pulled by harnessed animals, such as the fine matched pair of white horses that brought Rica Dahlstrom and Miss Gordon to Junction City. The automobile was still a rich man's toy.
The Bumsteads posed proudly with theirs for the photographer. A crank inserted in the side (note the hole below the seat) started the car. The bicycle was an invention not much older than the auto, and most people thought it had a greater future. Pennell photographed Mr. Bush crossing Main Street.

78.

In October of 1900 there was neither auto nor bicycle to be seen in the business district of Junction City, just parking spaces filled by buggies and wagons and one man turning into the alley with a load of building stone. But Junction City was up-and-coming: it had electricity, a daily newspaper—the Tribune*—and a proud new limestone courthouse with a tower. Americans have always wanted to pinpoint their origins, so the building next to the* Tribune *office has its erection date on the cornice and, painted on the* Tribune *wall, is the information: "Established 1873." Twenty-five years made a tradition on the prairie.*

FRANCES BENJAMIN JOHNSTON:

In 1899 Frances Benjamin Johnston (1864–1952), the Washington society photographer who photographed the Lynn, Massachusetts, mill girls, was asked to take photographs of Hampton Institute in Virginia. Hampton Institute had been founded as a vocational school for Negroes and American Indians after the Civil War. One of its most famous graduates was Booker T. Washington, the best known Negro of his generation and the founder, in his turn, of Tuskegee Institute in Alabama. In 1902, with her photo-essay on Hampton having been a great success at the Paris Exposition of 1900, Frances Johnston went on to photograph Tuskegee Institute, built on Hampton's model. Tuskegee had been founded in 1881 when Booker T. Washington was called to be the principal of a vocational school for blacks in Macon County, Alabama. When Washington arrived, he found that the school had no teachers, no pupils and just a shanty for a schoolroom. He spent one summer canvassing the county for students and support. As soon as the school was functioning, in some fashion, with a second teacher and orderly classes, Washington began a campaign for funds. He was a pragmatist who was determined to help the American Negro achieve self-respect; and he worked with white people as circumstances demanded, agreeing to the principle of segregation in order to win support. Eventually, the support Washington got—from Andrew Carnegie, Theodore Roosevelt and J. P. Morgan, among others—was vastly increased by the publication in 1901 of his autobiography, *Up From Slavery*. By the time Frances Johnston went to Tuskegee, the school was educating 1200 Negro men and women in forty-two buildings on 2000 acres of land.

George Washington Carver, the foremost agricultural scientist in the United States and a Negro, headed Tuskegee's Department of Agriculture. Farmers of both races attended yearly conferences where they were advised how to get the most out of their thin topsoil that had been depleted by years of cotton-growing. Carver coaxed 266 bushels of sweet potatoes per acre from the land, instead of the 37 bushels local farmers had been getting; and he even managed to double the cotton crop.

Tuskegee's impact on the entire Negro population of the county, adults as well as students, was profound. When Washington went to Tuskegee, rural blacks still lived very much as they had under slavery. Their homes were shacks constructed of cast-off lumber, or even old slave cabins. They barely scraped a living from the soil—usually owned by whites—which they farmed for a share of the crops. Black people had no more chance for family life or its rituals, such as eating meals together, than they had when they were at the mercy of their masters' whims. One of Washington's counsels to the black farmers he encountered was to buy land and build a settled, stable way of life whenever possible. "Buy a hundred acres," he told them, "and if you can't do that, buy ten and if you can't do that make a start with one."

Washington's efforts to give the Negro a stake in his community and increased motivation for self-improvement kept Tuskegee primarily a vocational school. There was a wheelwright and wagon shop, cobbler shops, furniture shops and dressmaking and cooking classes, although academic work and classes in etiquette and manners played a large part in the curriculum. Washington's students teased him about the "gospel of the toothbrush"—his fanatical insistence on cleanliness. The etiquette and the emphasis on hygiene were all part of Washington's plan of making the Negro proud of himself as well as self-sufficient. Despite a constant demand for servants from white families, Tuskegee never supplied any from its cooking and sewing classes. There is today much question about Booker T. Washington's methods; and many contemporary black spokesmen feel that his emphasis on trades and domestic training as well as his lip service to segregation kept blacks in a subservient position. But even the wooden dummies in Tuskegee's millinery classes came painted with white skins; there was no letup to the reminders that it was a white man's world. And Booker T. Washington cooperated, as he had to, in order to give the Negro his first toehold.

Students at Tuskegee did all the construction work on campus. When Frances Johnston was there, the school was in a turmoil of digging and bricklaying. She camouflaged all this behind the careful composition of her photographs: even down to the position of tools and the rows of empty seats, each element in her photographs is a carefully placed part of the whole. The effect is a serene evocation of dignity and order. Those two qualities were essential to the new life Booker T. Washington wanted to offer the black people. When we compare the photographs Frances Johnston had taken of rural blacks who survived in patience and poverty with her firm, clear view of Tuskegee's activities, we realize on the one hand the depth of Washington's achievement and, on the other, the sensitivity of this photographer.

80

79.

The land in Macon County, Alabama, in 1902 was still given over to " King Cotton." The soil was depleted and the average farmer raised only 200 pounds— instead of a possible 500—to the acre; at the cotton gin weighing station there was a scene decades old: mules, cotton, a general store and black workers, with a white man doing the weighing.

80.

Sorghum, a grain from which sugar was extracted, was one of the South's staple sweeteners. The old man holds a barrel of raw sorghum, which has been pressed and strained through the burlap, and the juice now drains into troughs.

81.

The hope of deprived black people for a better life seemed to survive through years of grinding effort. An old woman, much like the one Frances Johnston photographed, came to Booker T. Washington when he was building Tuskegee and offered him six eggs—the only savings she had.

82.

In her country photographs, Frances Johnston was sensitive to the sources of Tuskegee—and black—potential. The school's students came from such proud people as the woman standing at her weathered gatepost.

83.

Church for rural black people was the same welcome weekly social occasion that it was for all isolated farm families in the years before the automobile. These people, in Sunday-go-to-meeting clothes, gather to talk after the service.

84.
Mt. Meigs Institute, one of Tuskegee's daughter schools, was housed in a frame building similar to that in which Tuskegee began. Everything, from the bell on the platform to the pupils' painstaking cleanliness, bespeaks the school's high purpose.

85–96

Tuskegee combined vocational studies, academics and outright maintenance work, with which the students paid for their educations. When Tuskegee had first outgrown its original wooden buildings, Booker T. Washington built three unsuccessful brick kilns. He had to pawn his watch to get material for a fourth, but it was successful. After that, students made bricks and constructed all school buildings themselves.

85

86

87

88

89

90

97.
There was a criticism that Tuskegee taught students trades, such as shoemaking, that were already obsolete in an industrial society. But the principal goal was to create social and economic opportunities for the black man in his own rural community.

91

92

93

94

95

96

E.J. BELLOCQ:

In the 1870's, when railroad men on the Kansas prairies visited "fancy ladies" in the local brothels, they would leave their red signal lights outside the house. This, according to some, was how the term "red-light district" came to designate an area of town where prostitutes lived and plied their trade. Across the United States, despite almost universal official condemnation, prostitution flourished in the "Tenderloin," "Skid Row" or "Barbary Coast" of every town from New York to San Francisco. Saloon girls were among the first women to settle the mining towns of the West. In Denver, before the turn of the century, the madams were a power in civic affairs; and in Omaha, Nebraska, at the same time, the best residential boulevard was lined with substantial citizens' homes on one side and a row of brothels on the other. Conditions varied for the girls in the houses. Some girls, such as the ones in mining camps, undoubtedly wanted to be where they were. The free life offered an alternative to the tedious respectability of small towns, where before World War I women had few rights and little independence unless they became schoolmistresses. On the other hand, many brothel inmates were farm or factory girls who had gone into city dance halls, been seduced by some nameless man, and were ashamed to go home again. Society and, often, the victim of a seduction concurred in feeling she was a damaged human being who could no longer mingle with decent people. In any contest with the law, the "bad" woman was publicly branded and punished, while the men involved, who were allegedly unable to control their brute natures—and might be prominent men in town besides—remained anonymous. Laconic notices, such as the one in a Pennsylvania village newspaper in 1913, reported that "Seven Women and Fifteen Men Caught in Raids Saturday Night—Spend Night in Borough Lock-up . . . Queen Brown, landlady of a house on an alley near Tenth Street was fined $7.72 . . . Nearly all of the men caught in these houses gave fictitious names." Regardless of her reason for being in a brothel, a girl had no easy time once she was there. The establishments, across the nation, varied from parlor houses where a lady's "favors" could cost as much as fifty or sixty dollars, to Western houses where customers bought brass checks for fifty cents entitling them to ten minutes with a "boarder." Some "boarders" turned in as many as fifty checks after a night's work. A doctor who made a study of prostitutes in the 1850's maintained that the "average duration of [professional] life among these women does not exceed four years from the beginning of their career." The awful monotony of the aimless days combined with hectic nights exacted a toll; and few girls had the strength or looks to work beyond the age of twenty-five.

RED LIGHT DISTRICT

One of the few places in the United States where prostitution was legal, and where brothel life assumed the level of a culture, was New Orleans. With its French and Spanish background, the river city was more open about prostitution than most of Anglo-Saxon Victorian America. In the days of slavery, there had been elegant quadroon balls in New Orleans, where beautiful mulatto courtesans and even respectable black families presented their daughters for young white planters to choose as mistresses. When the slave-based economy broke down after the Civil War, few had the money to maintain a mistress in her own residence, and the quadroon balls were replaced by open brothels, with white men seeking out white prostitutes and black men restricted to their own women. By the 1890's, the chill wind of Northern morality had blown down across New Orleans and an alderman named Sidney Story proposed that prostitution be restricted to a few blocks along the waterfront. The area, called Storyville, existed from 1896 to 1917. It was in the bars and bordellos of Storyville that jazz evolved. And when the secretary of the navy closed Storyville, hundreds of out-of-work New Orleans jazz musicians migrated north, introducing their music to new audiences in Memphis, St. Louis and Chicago.

E. J. Bellocq (c. 1875–c. 1940),who photographed the women of Storyville, was a small man with an enlarged, oddly shaped head—the result of a condition known as encephalitis, or "water on the brain." He was a professional photographer for ship-building companies and at times he worked as a mechanic. Very little is known about him, partly because he was sensitive about his appearance, and the prostitutes whom he photographed may have been his only friends; there is an openness in their faces that suggests that they regarded him as an intimate and a familiar presence. The idea of a deformed man creating sensitive portraits of brothel inmates, whom he knew as companions, recalls Toulouse-Lautrec, the French painter who worked in Paris in the 1890's.

Although the standards of feminine beauty have changed since 1912, when the hourglass figure was the sexual ideal, the accoutrements such as black stockings and drapery are still alluring. These women seem content, and some are quite beautiful. Whether it is Bellocq's vision or the relative freedom of their lives in New Orleans that gives his women their serenity, they remain mysterious, beckoning to us from another age as they beckoned to customers from the gaslit rooms of Storyville.

98

98–102.

Bellocq's harlots confront the camera surrounded by all the paraphernalia of respectable Victorian virgins: Spanish shawls, paper flowers, chaste statuary, oriental rugs and wicker couches. In his novel Sanctuary, *William Faulkner describes a room in a southern brothel that might be the one where Bellocq's girl in the striped stockings sits. "The dressing-table was littered with toilet articles tied in pink satin bows. The mantel supported a wax lily beneath a glass bell; above it, draped in black, the photograph of a meek looking man with an enormous moustache. On the walls hung a few lithographs of spurious Greek scenes, and one picture done in tatting . . ." Bellocq's girl added a bottle of whiskey and miniature rocking chairs tipped with feathers to set them rocking in the slightest breeze. The girls seem almost to parody fashionable affectations; the one in the black stockings and the one wearing the body stocking display their perfect hour-glass figures that every decent woman strove for with corsets; and the nude girl languishes on her wicker daybed like all popular tubercular Victorian heroines. In the photographs the women retain the mystery they had for many upstanding citizens of the time; we find it hard to imagine them speaking—or how they filled the long afternoons that preceded their raucous nights.*

ERWIN SMITH.

The American frontier is supposed to have officially disappeared in December of 1890,
when Chief Sitting Bull was shot to death by United States cavalry officers
at the Battle of Wounded Knee. The "savages" were tamed then, and all the land in the
territorial United States was now available to the white man. But eras don't end
quite so neatly; and the figure of the frontiersman, which had grown to mythic
proportions in the American imagination—from Daniel Boone to Kit Carson—lingered
on in reality well into the 20th century. The characteristics that distinguished
the frontiersman were, simultaneously, love of freedom and pride in some work
that pitted his skills and cunning against the wilderness. The work could be fur trapping
or hunting or, later on, cow-punching and even logging. All these ways of life
involved wresting a living from the land without tying yourself to it; the farmer wanted
to consider the land a partner but the frontiersman knew it as an adversary.
Unfortunately for us, few photographs remain of the early frontiersmen, but two
photographers, Darius Kinsey and Erwin Smith, did record the last frontiers of logging
and cow-punching.
Erwin Smith (1886–1947), who left more than 1800 negatives of cowboys at their
work, was born in Texas and was inspired by the romance of the open range
when he visited his uncle's ranch in 1894 at the age of eight. He later went back to
work there in the summer and bought a small camera. Smith could step from the relative
civilization of Bonham, Texas, where his stepfather was the richest merchant in
town, to the ranch and back again. Consequently, he never quite settled in either place
and, like Solomon Butcher, he never quite belonged to the world he lived in and
photographed. Originally he had wanted to be a sculptor of the cowboy; when he was
eighteen he went to Chicago to study with Lorado Taft, a sculptor and art
historian. After two years he was going on to study in Boston, when he realized that
the range was disappearing so fast that there soon wouldn't be anything left there to
sculpt. "I knew that the life wouldn't wait," he said, "and that the technique
would."
The life that wouldn't wait had already, in fact, changed radically. From 1860 to 1890,
cattlemen let their animals graze and roam between Texas and Montana over
the unfenced government land called the open range. They branded them with the mark
of their ownership and rounded them up when it was time to drive them to
the slaughterhouses. But by the 1890's almost a million and a half new farms had been
established on 400 million acres of plains land and fenced off with barbed wire.
The ranchers, bitterly opposing the "sod-busters'" settlements, were nonetheless forced

THE COWBOY

to fence in their own land. So, by the time of Smith's photographs, cowpokes were working on ranches rather than on a thousand miles of open country. Smith, with his Eastman Kodak camera strapped to his horse, along with his saddle and bedroll, worked with the cowboys on the larger ranches—where life at least approximated conditions on the open range. In the evenings he would make sketches, roughing out the composition of the photographs he hoped to take. He had to base such compositions on what he thought was likely to happen, since the men and cattle in a roundup could hardly stop to pose for him. One observer at a roundup reported that Smith "rode past at a dead run, raced to the top of a rocky hill, dismounted, dropped his bridle reins in true cowboy fashion, and was ready to photograph the herd as the boys pushed them across Parker Creek and corraled them in the branding pen."

The photographs he took with such sympathy for the movements of men and beasts are themselves extremely evocative of motion. They frame the fluid grace of a lasso or a rearing horse; in some pictures cattle restlessly dot the entire surface. The constant activity of life among a herd of animals, with fires flickering and men moving around checking the shifting beasts, is caught in the photographs—as though the viewer could look away and when he looked back the action would have shifted. Smith's photographs, even when they are arranged, deal exclusively with action so that they are like scenes from a movie that has just been stopped for a moment.

In Smith's later years he went bankrupt, and the West that he loved was increasingly to be found only at the movies. But for all his romance about the cowboy, Smith never cared much for the Hollywood western. For him, the cowboy was "a man with a job to do," and that was one thing the vagrant cowpoke in the movie versions never did.

103.
There were two roundups on the open range, one in the spring for counting the herd and branding the calves, and one in the fall for selecting the cattle to be driven to the railroad and the stockyards.

104.
The dust on the range was scarcely assuaged by the shallow rivers where the cattle were allowed to rest.

105.

"Cutting out"—that is, separating—a calf from the herd for branding demanded great skill on the part of the rider and his horse. It was important not to excite the rest of the herd or the mother cow (possibly lowering her horns) or a stampede might result.

106–107.

Once the calf was roped it had to be "flanked"—that is, thrown on its side and held down to be branded. The operation required strength and perfect timing.

Any male calf not worthy to become a breeder was castrated at this point as well as branded—thus becoming a steer.

108.

*After breakfast the cowboy chose his mount for the day
from the* remuda, *the herd of available horses. Even
horses that were completely broken in often got
"spooky" when saddled and tried to throw their riders off.*

109.

It often took two men to lasso a rebellious horse; and the job had to be done several times a day, since cowboys needed three or four fresh mounts if no horse was to be overworked.

110.

The center of the camp was the portable kitchen called the "chuck wagon," where the camp cook, usually an old cowboy and a vital member of the work force, prepared the heavy meal, steak or stew, for noon. (Note the time, 10:10, on the clock between the mugs and coffee cans.) Men who had worked during the night dozed while the cook clattered his pot lids.

111.

After supper around the campfire, the only entertainment was telling tall tales. A cowhand got as good at cutting out truth from fiction as he was at cutting out calves from a herd.

ADAM VROMAN:

Few of the photographers who worked at recording an American way of life were
aesthetes—or people who saw the situations they photographed as raw material for art.
One exception, however, was Adam Vroman (1856–1916), a prosperous bookstore
owner who collected first editions and Japanese netsuke, the tiny carved jade
and ivory figures with which the Japanese fastened a kimono sash. A man of delicate
and precise tastes, Vroman's approach to the Southwest Indians was that of the
collector and explorer. When he set out in the early 20th century to photograph the
Indians, he saw them as a self-contained culture with their own rituals and forms
within the Anglo-Saxon domain of America; and, consequently, his pictures are
remarkably free of the standard American prejudices about the Indian. Vroman's Hopi
and Zuñi are not the wild horsemen of the plains, living in teepees and wearing
feathered war bonnets, practicing barbaric rites. The people in these photographs are
farmers and villagers living in permanent settlements that might be poor
communities in Spain or southern Italy; they practice complex religious ceremonies
that, again, seem to be the counterparts of Mediterranean feast days.
The Hopi and the Zuñi are descendants of foraging Indians who began to settle in
villages and cultivate the land around 300 B.C. The Southwest was as arid then as it is
now. It is conjectured, however, that the very hostility of the area fostered agriculture,
because the foraging was so poor for men—and for the beasts that the men hunted—
that plant life had to be nurtured. At first these farmers depended heavily on
foraging and hunting to supplement their diets, but by A.D. 1000 agriculture was a way
of life. The ancestors of the present-day Hopis also became architects, building
awesomely placed sandstone pueblos into the cliffs. Life in the cliff dwellings
ended about 1300, probably because of a generation-long drought. After a long period
of wandering, the Indians had migrated only a few hundred miles. They settled and
their descendants taught other tribes to build the pueblos that Vroman
visited centuries later.
Vroman, who had been born in Illinois and had worked for a railroad company, began
his collection of Japanese netsuke at the age of 27, signaling his interest in the
subtleties of exotic civilizations. In 1894 he opened a bookstore in Pasadena, California,
which prospered almost immediately and freed him for photography. The next
year he made his first expedition to the Hopi village of Walpi, Arizona Territory, where
he photographed the snake ceremony. He also began to take photographs to serve
as illustrations for Helen Hunt Jackson's novel *Ramona*, which Mrs.
Jackson hoped would do for the Indians what *Uncle Tom's Cabin* had done for the

THE INDIAN

slaves. In the next nine years, Vroman returned again and again to the Southwest Indians.

The pueblo tribes, whom Vroman photographed between 1897 and 1904, were the poverty-stricken victims of white expansionism. The United States Bureau of Indian Affairs had, at one time or another, waged war on them, subjected them, as in the case of the Navajos, to forced starvation marches to a strange territory, and restricted several tribes to a single reservation in an arid land. The Hopi and the Zuñi were settled tribes who depended on an economy of corn agriculture and, although they had always managed to scrape survival from the desert, they could not withstand the intrusion of the Navajos onto their land and the relentless economic and cultural assaults of the white bureaucracy.

The Southwest tribes had a complex and private religious life, carried on in the kivas—secret underground rooms—of their ancient stone pueblos. In their villages of rock and adobe, stacked on top of mesas for defense, they had to cope with tourists, self-righteous missionaries and insensitive anthropologists. Because they were a settled agricultural people and so, of course, easily accessible, the pueblo-dwellers were especially vulnerable to the Bureau of Indian Affairs and the tourist. The Indians were particularly wary of photographers, whom they called "shadow catchers": capturing a man's image was thought to give whoever held the photo control of the subject's spirit. They also feared that the photographs of the religious ceremonies would be used by the bureau to prohibit or alter such practices. Vroman at first had to woo the Hopi into letting him photograph them. He would let them look through the camera at him, and then they would usually agree to reverse the positions. His photographs do not present the Indians as a sideshow, hostile or entertaining, to American life, but as people worthy of respect and attention in themselves. From the earlier photographs, which give an outsider's view, to the later ones, showing intimate details such as how the "squash-blossom" hairdo is achieved, he deals with them as people whom he respected and had come to consider his friends.

114

115

116

117

118

119

120

121

112.

Walpi village was one of the Hopi pueblos situated on top of a mesa. The village was built in the style the Hopi had used for more than five hundred years. These villages could be reached only by narrow, breakneck paths up the face of the cliffs; in some places ladders were necessary. Villagers made the climb several times daily to and from their fields in the more fertile creek bottoms.

113.

Vroman's intimacy with his subject, increased sharply in the years he took their pictures; no photographer afterward received such cooperation. These young men wear white men's suspenders and jeans, but the silver belt and the girls' "squash blossom" hairdos are traditions that are at least eight hundred years old.

114–121,

The "squash blossom" hairdo, the badge of unmarried girls, required elaborate construction on a reed frame. Young girls wore it from puberty. They were courted when they went to the village well: a suitor asked his favorite girl for a drink, if she gave him one he would ask her father for her hand.

122.

Only men, in Hopi society, did the weaving, and often they removed themselves to the circular, sacred underground chambers called kivas *to do so.*

123.

The climax of the Hopi year was either the Snake Festival or the Flute Festival. Held alternate years at the end of summer, they sought the gods' favor and enough rain to survive in the arid land. The ceremonies were emotional and religious purgings that unified the tribe and gave them new purpose. The Flute Festival was the more sacred. It involved two societies, the "Blue Flute" and the "Drab Flute"; both groups can be seen in Vroman's photograph. There were eight days of secret observances in the kivas *before the public ceremony on the ninth day. The circles on the ground have been drawn in sacred oatmeal by the priests; and the three figures at the front of each group are two maidens and a young boy, who represent the ancestral heroes of the Flute societies.*

Because of insensitive photographers and spectators, everyone except the Hopi themselves were eventually banned from these religious festivals.

122

124

124.

The Zuñi are a pueblo Indian people who live today in a single community in New Mexico. Their way of life was agricultural and much like that of the Hopi. Zuñi women carried water in clay vessels called ollas.

125.

The pueblos of the Rio Grande were made up of Indians from various tribes, and because of long years of relatively peaceful coexistence with the Spanish and Mexicans, there was even some intermarriage between peoples of the pueblos and the white settlements. José Leandro Tofoya, photographed with his grandchildren, had some Spanish blood; he was the United States "governor" of Santa Clara Pueblo. The "governors" of the pueblos were administrative Indians responsible to the government rather than to the tribe.

EDWARD CURTIS:

The Indians that Edward Curtis (1868–1952) photographed were living out the last days of cultures that had originated in the return of the horse in 1518. Before that time the nomadic plains Indians, who were the greatest beneficiaries of the animal's strength, could move possessions only on their own backs, or with dogs. This vastly limited the size of teepees and the number of permanent possessions a tribe could accumulate. The horse could move bigger lodges and the inhabitants had more leisure to enjoy them. The difference between hunting a buffalo on foot, which entailed many men driving the animal toward a pit that had been dug earlier, and hunting one on horseback was the difference between a few hours' effort with pretty certain success and days of labor. With increased leisure and mobility, as well as wealth, there was time and reason for warfare, so plains societies grew complex and ritualized. Prestigious horsed warrior castes set the tone for the tribes.

In the popular imagination the Indian is associated as much with horses as with peace pipes and scalps. And yet, until recently scholars thought that, like peace pipes and the practice of taking scalps, the horse was brought to this continent by the white man. The first horses were supposed to have come with Cortez to Mexico in 1518. In fact, it is now known that the horse is a far older inhabitant of America than any man, white or red. The ancestor of all horses in the world was born here; and the small prehistoric animal made several trips across the shifting bridge of ice and land between Alaska and Siberia while the ancestors of the Indian were crossing that land bridge toward America. About 12,000 years ago, long after the Indians had permeated the American continent, the last American prehistoric horses died out, while the Asian ones flourished. The Indians, at some primeval time, had known horses here—although only as game animals.

When the Spanish conquistadors appeared in the 16th century, all memory of the horse had vanished; and the first mounted men appeared to be nine-foot gods or war machines, moving like the wind and equally terrifying to sophisticated Aztec foot soldiers and primitive nomadic hunters. Nevertheless, in 1594, seventy-six years after the reintroduction of the horse to this continent, an exploring Spanish friar records that in northern Mexico an Indian chief, who had never seen any white men, came to meet him on horseback. By 1600 the horse had become essential to Indian ways of life as far south as what is now Argentina and as far north as New Mexico.

Edward Curtis was a photographer who immersed himself in American Indian life. So it is appropriate to publish as an example of his work photographs of Indians

THE INDIAN ON HORSEBACK

on horseback. Over a twenty-three-year period, he ultimately published forty volumes of photographs on the Indians and all their activities. As well as being a professional photographer, he had the instincts of an anthropologist and an urgent sense of the Indians' imminent cultural destruction.

He had begun his work in 1893 when he opened a studio in Seattle and had enough leisure to do photographic studies of the Indians around Puget Sound. After expanding his plan of photographing Indian life into a five or six year project, which would culminate in several volumes on the subject, Curtis realized that he must have financial backing. He managed to work seven years until, in 1905, with the project still in no way approaching completion, he wrote to President Theodore Roosevelt begging help. Roosevelt replied with an enthusiastic letter, which he urged Curtis to use as a recommendation. Spurred on, Curtis turned to J. Pierpont Morgan, the philanthropist and financier, who, with surprising alacrity, agreed to put up $75,000 in return for twenty-five of the proposed fifteen hundred sets of books in the first published edition. Morgan died in 1913, but Curtis was bringing out volumes every year and Morgan's son agreed to continue his subsidy. Finally, with a price of $3500 per set, all forty volumes of *The North American Indian* were available in 1930. Curtis, after more than thirty years of the most intense involvement and effort, collapsed into a two-year mental breakdown. He survived, however, to live on well into his eighties.

By the time Curtis photographed his subjects riding silently across canyons or disappearing over ledges, their backs to the camera, they were a beleaguered breed. Just as the horse as a transport and pack animal had changed the Indians' lives three hundred years before, so the railroad—an iron horse—made the plains accessible to the white man and changed the Indians' lives again. Only this time the change was to the advantage of another people and contributed to the near extinction of the red man.

In 1905, when Theodore Roosevelt had written encouraging Edward Curtis, he said Curtis's work was particularly valuable because "the Indian, as an Indian, is on the point of perishing, and when he has become a United States citizen, although it will be a much better thing for him and for the rest of the country, he will lose completely his value as a living historical document." Curtis worked desperately against time to record the last people on the continent to whom animals were more important than machines; and the nation's president and the nation's biggest financier paid huge sums to commemorate the people whom their civilization helped exterminate.

126–130.

The Navaho Indians on horseback, whom Curtis photographed, shared the arid Southwest with the settled pueblo farmers, the Hopi and the Zuñi. The Navahos had come into the Southwest from Canada around the time of the Spanish conquest. They were related to the Apache and shared their predilection for raiding the communities of the whites and pueblo Indians.
The Navahos also raised sheep—brought by the Spaniards —but they mainly saw themselves as a warrior people. Their semi-nomadic life with their flocks and the raids were both possible because of the horse. The image Curtis caught of mysterious, blanket-draped Indians riding silently through vast canyons, or stopping by a

pond to listen for footfalls, fulfilled the picture the white man had of the wily savages. The Navahos were proud of this view of themselves, as they were proud of outwitting the invaders of their land.

ARNOLD GENTHE:

A German scholar from a family of the *haute bourgeoisie*, Arnold Genthe (1869–1942) came to San Francisco in its ostentatious 1890's as a tutor to the son of a German baron and a California heiress. Genthe, who stood six-foot-two "in his riding boots" and had aquired a Ph.D. with a thesis in Latin on philology, was a romantic figure who responded to the fascination of San Francisco's Chinatown. On evenings when he was free, he would wander around, unnoticed as any "foreigner" inevitably was by the ethnocentric Chinese. But when he tried to sketch some of the mystery and bustle of those eight square city blocks, the street would empty, as the Chinese believed that anyone who took their image could work evil with it. At last Genthe bought a small camera with a Zeiss lens, "a black devil box" according to the Chinese, but at least less obvious than a sketch pad. He lurked in doorways and ducked behind pillars, taking photographs until he had captured images of this murky, self-contained world—reputedly full of slave girls and opium dens—off Portsmouth Square.

After his tutoring job ended, Genthe decided to stay in America and become a professional photographer. San Francisco society ladies brought their children and friends for photographs and his career was launched. Typical of his life-style was his insistence during the San Francisco earthquake on rushing into his home— which was about to be dynamited—so he could retrieve a bottle of Johannisberger Schloss '93 from his wine cellar, while ignoring his entire collection of prints and negatives. The collection perished. All that remained of the photographic work he had done before 1906 was the Chinatown series, which had been stored at a friend's house outside the city.

The first Chinese had come to California in the 1850's—calling themselves "Gum Shan Hok," Guests of the Golden Mountain—for the same reason as everyone else: gold. They were mostly men who had left their families in the farmlands around Canton, fully intending to return when they had made their fortunes. They arrived in California only to discover that they were legally—and forcibly—banned from the digging. So they opened restaurants, washed laundry and, in 1864, proved more efficient and less rowdy than anybody else wielding a pick and shovel on the Central Pacific Railroad.

By 1880 the population of California was 865,000, of whom 75,000 were Chinese. San Francisco's Chinatown had a population that ranged between 10,000 and 30,000, depending on whether the railroads were hiring and the northern canneries were in operation. Chinatown was a highly structured community, under the unofficial

CHINATOWN

government of the Chinese merchant organization known as "The Six Companies."
However, despite their industry and relatively peaceful behavior, they were not
allowed to vote, become citizens, use the city hospital, testify in court or send their
children to school. The ghetto situation of the Chinese and their view of themselves as
temporary residents among barbarians combined to create a tightly knit, closed
society. After the Chinese Exclusion Act of 1882, when virtually no Chinese were allowed
to enter the United States, Chinatown drew in and literally dug deeper and deeper
(sometimes three levels below a building) into the earth. Being the most noticeable alien
culture in California made the Chinese in San Francisco much more exotic than
were any of the many ethnic groups that crowded New York's Lower East Side. And
it was this aura of mystery that the tall German with his black devil box felt. In his
autobiography, Genthe remembers of Chinatown:"There was 'The Street of the
Gamblers' with its rows of sliding solid iron doors to be clanked swiftly shut at the
approach of the police or the threat of battle with a rival concessionaire. The smell of
the place—it was a mixture of the scent of sandalwood and exotic herbs from the
drugstores, the sickly sweetness of opium smoke, the fumes of incense and roast pork,
and the pungent odors from the sausages and raw meat hanging in the 'Street
of the Butchers.' And in the air there was always the sound of temple gongs, the clashing
of cymbals and the shrill notes of an orchestra . . ."

131.
Men in dark blue throng San Francisco Chinatown's
"Street of the Gamblers." The tension in the
overcrowded street seems greater when one realizes that
the Chinese might attack the photographer if they knew
he had taken a picture.

132.

Chinese merchants in America tried to reproduce as closely as possible the stock they sold in open markets in the Celestial Kingdom. But one businessman, writing advice to later immigrants, said, ". . . do not include rats among your inventory because it would be too expensive to import them. The rat which is eaten by the Chinese is a field animal which lives on rice, grain and sugar cane. Its flesh is delicious."

133.

Only once every seven years, at the Good Lady Festival, could Chinese women promenade freely in the streets. After the festival the banners bearing holy inscriptions and the gods' names were burned so they would not be defiled. The woman poking a burning remnant in the gutter is oblivious of the American who suspiciously watches her pagan rite.

134–135.

Children were treasured in Chinatown because most men originally did not bring families and few new immigrants could enter the United States after the Chinese Exclusion Act of 1882. The all-important family structure of the community depended on the small, solemn creatures who were dressed as tiny adults. The toy vendor's stall, babies and rattles to the contrary, conveys a certain menace. Is the vendor looking over his shoulder because he senses the photographer's camera that violates a taboo? The father's pigtail was a symbol of subjugation to the Manchu emperor in China; he wears it in America to show that he is not an occidental barbarian.

133

134

136.

The photographer's caption for the men reading the wall posters was "Reading the Tong Warnings." Chinatown was unofficially governed by a merchant council known as "The Six Companies," but gangs of thugs were employed to keep order. The gangs were called tongs; individual members were called "highbinders" (by occidentals), perhaps because they bound their pigtails up, so as not to be grabbed and held by the hair in a fight. The sleeves of the rich man reading the wall posters hang below his hands to show that he does not have to work.

DARIUS KINSEY:

The forests were always both a resource and a problem in America. In colonial
New England, squatters who owned no land could nonetheless make money from selling
the timber on land they cleared. One of the earliest clashes with England
came in 18th-century New Hampshire, when the king requisitioned all pine trees marked
by his woodsmen (which were valuable in local shipbuilding) for his own use as
masts on British navy vessels. On the other hand, the clearing of the forests of Ohio
and Kentucky, soon after 1800, was a national disgrace because settlers, too lazy to chop
down the trees, just girdled the trunks and waited for the trees to die. Until the
mid-19th century the prevailing attitude was that there were too many trees
and they had to be cleared, but they could usually be eliminated with a
profit. Then, with industry booming and settlers on the treeless prairies demanding
wood, logging became an industry in earnest, especially in the big woods of Wisconsin.
In the years after the Civil War, 120,000 lumberjacks were employed in the white pine
forests of Michigan and Wisconsin every winter. Lumbering was a rough business,
described as "dripping with blood." Chopped-off fingers, mangled limbs
and broken backs were common results of the drive to fell the trees; and most of the
lumberjacks, penniless immigrants without families, had nothing to lose in fights with
each other except a few day's pay. For a dollar a day, payable in the spring at
the end of the season, the woodsmen cut down the trees, sawed them into lengths that
sawmills could handle and hitched them behind horses or oxen, which towed
them over an iced "skid road" to a river bank. When the river ice broke up in the
spring, the logs were lashed together into rafts and floated down to a sawmill. (In time,
"skid road" also came to refer to the street in a sawmill town where the
lumberjacks' bars and brothels were located, and eventually it was applied to any
district of down-and-outers.) This fraternity of rough-living men devastated
the pine forests of the North Central states, creating along the way the legends of the
giant logger, Paul Bunyan. By the 1890's stumps, with gulleys eroded between them,
were all that remained of vast stands of trees.
Just about that same time, in 1891, a young Missouri man, Darius Kinsey (1871–1945),
went to Snoqualmie, Washington, to photograph the lumbermen who were
making a stand against the last frontier of giant fir, cedar and redwood trees in the
Pacific Northwest. Kinsey and his brother built a hotel in Snoqualmie. But Darius, with
time on his hands, took photography lessons in Seattle and in 1892 set out with
his $6\frac{1}{2}'' \times 8\frac{1}{2}''$ camera to the lumber camps that were within reach of Puget Sound steamers

IN THE BIG WOODS

and the independent railroads. Later he bought an old boxlike wagon and a horse that he could use for travel on the "skid roads" from camp to camp. "You aren't a logger," he would tell the lumberjacks, "until you own a dollar watch and have your picture taken with a tree."

In 1896 Kinsey married and moved to the town of Sedro Woolley. There he set up a studio and remained for the rest of his life. Like Bennett in the Wisconsin Dells, Kinsey had to do portrait work and commercial photography to survive, but his vocation lay in photographing the rough-and-tumble men out there in the woods.

Kinsey was a strict Methodist, and his slogan, "We will photograph anything, anywhere, anytime, except on Sunday," is of a piece with the self-portrait in which he stands, stiff and straight in a derby hat and celluloid collar, surrounded by the tools of his trade. Kinsey believed in a day's work for a day's pay, and old men still living in that part of Washington, who as boys carried his equipment, say that no one ever carried it twice because it was so much work. After fifty years of photographing the lumberjacks, Kinsey died of a fall from the top of a redwood stump where he had been taking a photograph.

Kinsey's pictures are thorough records of one of the last frontier encounters and of an early American industry. Kinsey's lumberjacks, like Erwin Smith's cowboys, were men with a job to do. Paradoxically, the lumbermen did not think that they were destroying natural resources or the wilderness; instead they thought they were clearing the way for civilization. Nevertheless, the Pacific Northwest of Kinsey's photographs could almost symbolize the monumental destruction that the settlers of America visited on the land for two hundred years. These cedars and firs are so huge that a single photograph generally shows nothing but a section of the trunk; they make the men look like insects. And yet, these tiny men, with axes like toys, turned the trees into piles of sticks at a sawmill. It was as though the land said: You have polluted the waters and slaughtered the passenger pigeons and ravaged the earth for its coal and iron, surely these trees are too big for you to destroy. But they were not.

137.

The lumber camps in Washington state were home to hundreds of men while they chopped down the forests. The mess hall of one camp had places set for 160 lumberjacks. In addition to unlimited cookies, one "jack" might eat sausage, cereal, eggs, a dozen flapjacks and pie for breakfast.

138.

When Kinsey began to photograph in 1892, he took a unique nighttime interior which he called "Loggers enjoying an evening in the BUNK HOUSE." Before the flash powder went off the only light in the crowded room came from a single kerosene lamp; after the flash went off, the smoke and smell probably drove the lumberjacks out into the snow.

138

139

139.

Every lumber camp had female cooks and miscellaneous children and dogs, and even a shy courting or two; but with only skid roads for miles around, where did the man ride his bicycle?

140.

"Fallers" were the men who actually felled a tree. They drove wedges in the trunk, on which they stood. They chopped an "undercut" that would control the direction the tree would fall. These six young men sit in a completed undercut. At the tree's other side, they sawed and then drove wedges through the trunk until the tree toppled in the direction of the original cut.

141.

An alternative to skid roads was a track made of logs that were too small to send to the mill. Manageable sections of wood, called "sawlog lengths," which had been cut by a man called a "bucker," were loaded onto horse-drawn cars with the aid of a primitive steam-powered windlass.

142.

If the grade down to the water or the mill was too steep for putting the logs on railroad cars (which might have broken away), an engine, such as the one owned by Knight's Lumber Company, dragged logs between the tracks as though the space were a skid road.

143

144

143.

Guiding a log jam down the river to a Puget Sound sawmill risked a man's limbs and possibly life, as he kept the logs moving with the current.

144.

Besides being put on railroad cars, or dragged, or floated down a river, logs were sometimes sent to a mill on a flume—a stream diverted into an inclined wooden trough. In the flume, logs could be floated on the rushing water without anyone guiding them. One planing and shingle mill was at the end of a three-mile-long flume, one section of which is at the upper right of the photograph.

145.

The use of wood was prodigal in the Pacific Northwest and there was no reason why the Pacific States Lumber Company should not build a temporary trestle 203 feet high and 893 feet long for their railroad from camp to mill. At the trestle's far side was an extra set of supports, called "bents," to protect the Seattle city water pipeline that ran under the trestle and along the hillside.

146.

Before the loggers got to them, the most magnificent trees in the world rose in the Pacific Northwest. The cedar in Kinsey's photograph, thousands of years old, might stand for the immensity of America's natural resources at one time. The girls celebrate its strength; and the people in the buggy might be looking back at the end of an era of natural abundance.

145

ACKNOWLEDGEMENTS:

The compilation of any book of old photographs such as *The Way Life Was* necessarily involves the help of many people who have taken, loved and kept the photographs. We particularly want to mention·our appreciation for the help of Robert Johnson of Culver Pictures, Jerry Kearns of the Library of Congress, Miss Charlotte La Rue of the Museum of the City of New York, Raymond Delgado of the Staten Island Historical Society, George Griffin of the Kansas Collection at the University of Kansas, Oliver Reese of the Bennett Studios, and Peggy Buckwalter of the American Heritage Publishing Company.

Some people who have been most helpful were not directly associated with collections of photographs, but their historical knowledge was invaluable. We are grateful to Samuel R. Spencer, whose book *Booker T. Washington and the Negro's Place in American Life* (Little, Brown and Company, Boston, 1955) provided background information for the essay on Frances Benjamin Johnston's photographs of Tuskegee Institute; and to Walter Trattner, whose book *Crusade for the Children* (Quadrangle Books, Chicago, 1970) furnished information about Lewis Hine.

Uniquely helpful was Miss Grace Mayer, whose book *Once Upon a City* (Macmillan Company, New York, 1958) makes public the photographs of Joseph and Percy Byron, as well as information about their lives and work.

There are a few people who graciously shared their specialized knowledge during the research and writing of *The Way Life Was*: Diana Edkins of the Photography Department of the Museum of Modern Art; Daniel W. Jones of Project 20, National Broadcasting Company; and Robert Weinstein of the Ward Ritchie Press, who is also the author and editor of *Dwellers at the Source* (Grossman Publishers, New York, 1973), a collection of the photographs of Adam Vroman.

We are grateful to the entire group of editors of the American Heritage Publishing Company, whose efforts over the years have been responsible for rescuing many of these photographers from obscurity and bringing them to the public eye.

CREDITS:

Illustrations 1–7, Culver Pictures; 8–12, Library of Congress; 13–21, Staten Island Historical Society; 22, Culver Pictures; 23–35, Museum of the City of New York; 36–46, Library of Congress; 47–53, H. H. Bennett Studios; 54–60, Solomon D. Butcher Collection, Nebraska State Historical Society; 61–70, Kansas State Historical Society; 71–78, Kansas Collection, University of Kansas; 79–97, Library of Congress; 98–102, Lee Friedlander (These photographs first appeared in *E. J. Bellocq: Storyville Portraits,* Museum of Modern Art, New York, 1970); 103–111, Erwin Smith Collection, Library of Congress; 112–113, Los Angeles County Museum; 114–121, Southwest Museum; 122–125, Los Angeles County Museum; 126–130, Library of Congress; 131–136, Museum of Modern Art; 137–146, Culver Pictures.

The editors are grateful for the permission to quote from the following works: *The Country of the Pointed Firs and Other Stories,* Sarah Orne Jewett; W. W. Norton and Company, Inc., New York, 1968. *How the Other Half Lives,* Jacob Riis; Dover Publications, Inc., New York, 1971. *The Age of Innocence,* Edith Wharton; New American Library, Inc., New York, 1961. *My Antonia,* Willa Cather; Houghton, Mifflin Company, Boston, 1954. *Main Street,* Sinclair Lewis; Harcourt, Brace, Jovanovitch, New York, 1948. *Sanctuary,* William Faulkner; Random House, New York, 1958.